WHEN YOU GROW UP TO VOTE

HOW OUR GOVERNMENT WORKS FOR YOU

★ ★ ★

WHEN YOU GROW UP TO VOTE

VOTE

HOW OUR GOVERNMENT WORKS FOR YOU

★ ★ ★

Eleanor Roosevelt

with Michelle Markel

Illustrated by *Grace Lin*

ROARING BROOK PRESS

NEW YORK

Thanks are owed to Mona Field, professor emeritus, political science, Glendale Community College, who helped me make this complex subject accessible to young readers. I'm also grateful to the mayor's office of the City of Los Angeles and to that city's police and fire departments, to the governor's office of the State of California, and to the F.B.I. for the information they provided. —M.M.

Published by Roaring Brook Press
Roaring Brook Press is a division of Holtzbrinck Publishing
Holdings Limited Partnership
175 Fifth Avenue, New York, NY 10010

mackids.com

Our books may be purchased in bulk for promotional, educational, or business use. Please contact your local bookseller or the Macmillan Corporate and Premium Sales Department at (800) 221-7945 ext. 5442 or by e-mail at MacmillanSpecialMarkets@macmillan.com.

First edition, 2018
Book design by Monique Sterling
Printed in China by RR Donnelley Asia Printing Solutions Ltd.,
Dongguan City, Guangdong Province

1 3 5 7 9 10 8 6 4 2

CONTENTS

INTRODUCTION
by Marian Wright Edelman

I am so grateful for the reissue of this wonderful book. Eleanor Roosevelt was a tireless and mighty moral warrior for peace and justice. She used her astute political skills and indomitable will to educate and move the country and world to help the neediest among us. Now her clear words, Michelle Markel's timely updates, and Grace Lin's charming new illustrations will help today's children understand who our local, state, and national elected officials are, what they do, and why it is so important for each of us to do our part to help choose them.

Beginning when my three sons were babies, my husband and I always took them with us when we voted so they could see and internalize democracy in action. It is so valuable for children to begin to understand how elections impact their health, education, safety, communities, nation, and world. In a democratic society, if we like or don't like what our political leaders are doing and stand for, then we must make that clear by using our voices and our votes. And children are never too young to learn that they, too, can make a difference.

Those of us who struggled and lived through the Civil Rights Movement know firsthand how fiercely and sacrificially many Black Americans fought and died for the right to vote not very long ago. One hundred years ago American women were still marching and fighting for equal voting rights that were not yet guaranteed by the Nineteenth Amendment. Around the world others are still struggling and sacrificing for a freedom too many Americans now take for granted or even neglect to use. We must always remember and teach children by our example that democracy is not a spectator sport and resist every effort to violate democratic processes, including the right to vote. Children will come away from this book excited that one day soon they will have the chance to use their own votes to help shape the world they want to live in.

Marian Wright Edelman is the founder and president of the Children's Defense Fund. She was the first black woman to be admitted to the Mississippi bar and has spent her career as an advocate for disadvantaged Americans. In 2000, she received the Presidential Medal of Freedom, the nation's highest civilian award.

FOREWORD
by Nancy Roosevelt Ireland

Eleanor Roosevelt and her granddaughter Nancy in 1961

Eleanor Roosevelt was one of the most important world leaders and human rights activists of the twentieth century, but to me she was simply "Grandmère." Even when I was a young child and she had many responsibilities, she always had time for me—she listened to me and took me seriously.

She had the special gift of making everyone she met feel as if she not only understood their lives but also cared for them individually.

She extended a sense of dignity to children. She believed they had rights in our democratic system and deserved to know how government worked. The original edition of *When You Grow Up to Vote* was published in 1932, the year my grandfather, Franklin Delano Roosevelt, was first inaugurated as president of the United States. The book was Eleanor's way of communicating to young people that they were an important part of our country. She was eager for them to reach the age when they could vote for themselves!

I'm delighted to introduce this updated version of *When You Grow Up to Vote* to a new generation of future voters. Even now, in this century, my grandmother's message of empowerment resonates.

Here is her hope for the young citizens of this great nation, in her own words:

Someday, perhaps in ten or twelve years, you are going to vote. You will help choose men and women to govern the country. But to vote well you will need to know about a great many things, interesting things.

Government is like a game. If you do not know the rules, or what each player is supposed to do, it is dull, but as soon as you understand what is going on, it can get very exciting.

Even now, you have been wondering about the President, the Governor, the Mayor, and other people in our government, what they do, and why we vote for them. You probably have a dozen questions all ready. I hope you will find the answers in this book.

—Eleanor Roosevelt, *When You Grow Up to Vote*
(1932)

Storage
(axes, extra hose,
traffic cones, and more)

Pump

Hose

Hook and
ladder

Sirens

Using a helicopter
to fight fires

Sliding down the pole

Rescuing people

— 1 —

FIRE! FIRE!

A fire engine goes barreling down the street, its sirens wailing. Inside the truck are firefighters willing to give their lives to protect us. These brave men and women put out fires and offer emergency medical response wherever it's needed—at the scene of accidents, natural disasters, even in your home. If you call, firefighters come. It's our government that makes this possible.

Every fire station has an engine to pump water and a hook and ladder to reach people trapped in tall buildings. Some stations have a vehicle for rescue, for cleaning up toxic spills, or for fighting wildfires. Some fire departments are even equipped with helicopters for reaching high-rises.

Helmet

Thick coat

Flashlight

Gloves

Ax

Breathing apparatus

Air tank

Reflective stripes

Compartment holding escape rope

Steel-toe boots

If you could be at an older fire station in the middle of the night when there was a fire, you would hear a loud bell to wake the firefighters on the second floor, then you would see them all slide down the pole and drive the engine out of the station—all in a minute or so. But many fire crews don't use poles. Newer stations are often one-story high.

Firefighters are proud of how swiftly they can get to a fire. They can usually put it out before it does much harm, as long as the alarm is sounded early enough. If you see a fire starting, be a good citizen and call 911— or if you're in a public place, pull the lever in the little fire alarm box. Fires are often caused by carelessness, so it's even more important to make sure you never accidentally start one yourself.

Managing crowds

Finding missing people

Radio

Cell phone

Baton

Pistol

Responding to accidents

Police dog

— 2 —

TO PROTECT
AND TO SERVE

A squad car races to the scene of an accident. When the police arrive, they have to move quickly—lives may be in danger and there's much to do! The officers check on the condition of the passengers, set down traffic cones to prevent a second car crash, inspect the evidence—maybe skid marks or broken glass—and finally clear the area so it's safe for motorists again. Like firefighters, the police are an important part of our government.

The police officer you've probably seen is a fit man or woman in uniform, equipped with a pistol, a baton, and in many cases a Taser and pepper spray. The officer has handcuffs, too, and a cell phone and a radio for contacting the police department. The police protect us in several ways—helping in local emergencies, managing crowds, finding missing people, issuing traffic tickets, and making arrests.

The part of the city that police patrol is called their beat, and they pursue anyone suspected of breaking the law there, even when they must risk their own lives to do so. Some officers take along a police dog to sniff for drugs, explosives, and even people.

Besides the uniformed officers, there are police detectives who investigate crimes. Outside the cities there are sheriffs, constables, state police, and national police called marshals and deputies—over one million officers altogether. One way they catch criminals is by entering scans of suspects' fingerprints into electronic databases. This system, run by the Federal Bureau of Investigation (FBI), identifies thousands of fugitives each month.

Flashing light

Police cruiser

The men and women in police uniforms have an important mission—to keep us safe.

Garbage collection team

Garbage truck with lift

Recycling

Stinky garbage

— 3 —

THE GARBAGE COLLECTOR

Perhaps you've been woken up by a rumbling, clanging sound and looked outside to see what's going on. It's the garbage collector, who drives a powerful truck that collects trash and recyclables from our neighborhoods. In some places, the garbage collector operates a lift, making its clawlike arm grab the trash container and hurl its contents up into the truck. In other places, garbage collectors work in teams—one driving the truck, the other stepping out to pick up and deposit the trash. Imagine how stinky and unsanitary our cities would be if nobody

collected our waste! We're lucky that our government is careful about our health, and keeps our streets and parks nice and clean.

Thank you, garbage collectors!

The Mayor

City councilors

works with the directors of

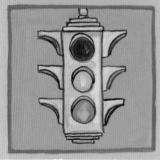

street maintenance,

animal regulation,

fire,

police,

parks,

building-code enforcement,

traffic control,

garbage collection,

and sometimes even more!

*Water, power, schools, libraries, and public transportation can be run by special departments.

4

THE HONORABLE MAYOR

You may have wondered who looks after all these things—who's in command of the police, who pays the firefighters and garbage collectors. In most U.S. cities and towns, it's a very busy person: the mayor! He or she works together with a council, whose members are all elected by the people. The council prepares rules, which become laws if the mayor approves them.

It's a big job to run a city—to make sure the buildings are safe, the streets paved, the traffic signals working, the trees trimmed, and much more. Mayors are too busy to take care of all this by themselves, so they appoint men and women to help them. We have directors for building safety, street maintenance, parks and recreation, libraries, animal control, and other departments. On a typical day, a mayor might meet with one or more of these directors on a matter of concern, take phone calls from the community, cut ribbons at the opening of a city project, give speeches to local groups, and attend receptions. It can be a long day!

The mayor leads the city and makes sure it's a safe, clean, pleasurable place to live.

At a New England town hall,

anyone can stand and speak.

At a county seat,

supervisors meet and
make decisions.

—5—

THE MEETING WILL COME TO ORDER!

Some cities choose not to have a powerful mayor. In that case, who's in charge? Sometimes it's the council members, who may also be known as alderpersons. Some cities have a manager instead of a mayor; others have a commission of five or seven people.

If you live in New England, the needs of your town are taken care of at a meeting. Once a year or so, voters come together in the town hall. Anyone may stand up and say what he or she thinks about roads, schools, a new roof for the firehouse, or anything else. And every person votes about what should be done. Voters may also decide whom they want for police or fire chief, and they choose representatives called selectpeople to govern the town for the following year.

What if your city, town, or village has no local government of its own? Then the county*—the part of the state where you live—looks after you. Several times a year, elected officials called county commissioners

or supervisors meet in the county seat, usually a large town. They make decisions about many things, such as taxes, roads, hospitals, water and electricity,

* In Louisiana a county is called a parish, and in Alaska, a borough.

and financial help for low-income people.

In some places, people are governed by cities but are served by counties, too. The county may be responsible for pros-

Sheriff

ecuting serious crimes, managing foster care for children, and keeping records of who is born and who dies. One of the most important people in the county is the police officer called the sheriff.

Another very important person is the county clerk, who keeps a record of your birthday—in case you've forgotten when it comes.

The
Governor

↑ Secretary
of State

↑ Lieutenant
Governor

↑ Attorney
General

↑ Treasurer

looks after the

farms,

factories,

forests,

and businesses

of the whole state!

6

AT THE STATEHOUSE

Cities and counties can settle their own private affairs, but there are many questions that are important to everyone in a state and that no mayor, council, or commission should decide alone. So each state elects a legislature to make laws and a governor to carry them out.

The legislature is made up of men and women from different parts of the state, some

elected to the state's Senate and some to the
state's House of Representatives—or Assembly. Each of us has a senator and at least one
representative at our statehouse whose job it
is to write laws. They work in separate cham-
bers in the state capitol.

The governor's job is like the mayor's, except that the governor is responsible for the whole state. Imagine all the work it takes to look after not only the farms, factories, and forests in a state but also the business that goes on in its cities. To help the governor there is a team of officials, some appointed and some elected. The attorney general, the top lawyer, decides on legal questions; the treasurer, or controller, manages the money the state must get and spend; and the secretary of state keeps records, runs elections, and certifies important papers with the state's great seal. Who takes over when the governor travels out of state? In most cases, it's the lieutenant governor.

Besides these men and women, there are heads of many state agencies, for instance, the Department of Agriculture, which inspects the safety of livestock and crops. The Department of Environmental Conservation protects energy, land, and mineral resources, and the Department of Public Works maintains highways, bridges, and other structures. Some states have more departments than others and call them by different names.

The state plays a role in almost everything we do. It makes sure that we go to school at least until we're old enough to get a job, that our workplaces are safe, and that when we drive a car we know how. The state has requirements for the dentist who looks after our teeth and for the nurse who gives us shots. Along with many other professionals, they must study, practice, and get a license in order to work.

Besides enforcing laws and appointing directors of agencies, governors have other powers and responsibilities. They come up with ideas for state projects. They can choose to pardon or shorten the sentences of certain criminals in prison, and to call out the

National Guard in case of an emergency or natural disaster. Governors have a lot to do and think about, and their decisions affect so many people!

The people choose the men and women who act at

City Hall,

the Statehouse,

and the Capitol Building.

— 7 —

WHY DO WE HAVE LAWS?

At home, you have rules you have to follow, even though you probably don't write them down. And at school, in offices, and in clubs we have rules, too. Wherever there is more than one person, we need rules or laws to prevent harm to one another and to avoid quarrels and confusion. The more people there are, usually the more rules there have to be. With more than 325 million people in the United States, we need quite a few rules for the whole nation.

For cities the laws are made by the members of councils or commissions, for the state they're written by the legislature, and for the nation they're made by the Congress—as you'll see in the next chapter. But it is always the people who make the laws because they choose the men or women who act for them in City Hall, in the Statehouse, and in the Capitol Building.

How do elected officials know what the voters want? They hear from organized groups called lobbies. Teachers have lobbies, and so do doctors and lawyers. Big businesses have lobbies; so do the workers they employ, and so do environmentalists and senior citizens. There are thousands of special interest groups, working every day, in every capital and major city, to persuade senators and congresspeople to pass laws that will benefit them.

Powerful lobbies host fund-raisers for legislators and make large contributions to their political campaigns—which can be very costly. Lawmakers repay them by meeting with those professional lobbyists, who argue their points of view. Lobbyists may even help write laws.

The problem is that our lawmakers need to hear the voices of all citizens, not just those of members of the best-run, most well-funded lobbies. Voters who don't belong to an interest group can still make a difference by taking part in a collective action. When a senator sees many constituents protesting at his or her office, hears them speak out at a town hall, or receives thousands of letters in favor of a certain law, he or she may be persuaded to vote for it.

Now, let's look at how a law is made.

HOW A LAW IS MADE

The idea for the law is written out in a certain way.

It is now a bill.

Then, the bill is voted upon either in the Senate or the Assembly (wherever the bill started). If it passes—if most of the members vote for it—it goes to the other house. If it passes there . . .

the bill goes to the governor.

If the governor refuses to sign (vetoes) it, it goes back to the Senate and Assembly, and two-thirds of the members of both houses must vote for it to become . . . a state law!

The bill is introduced to the state
Senate or State Assembly by one
of the members.

Sometimes the bill will be given a
public hearing, where anyone can say
what they think of the bill. Whatever
is said at the hearing can affect the
committees' amendments.

The bill goes to committee. The committee
considers the bill and possibly makes changes
to it, called amendments.

If the governor signs it, the bill becomes ...

a state law!*

*A federal, or national, law goes through the U.S. Senate and the U.S. House
of Representatives and is signed or vetoed by the president.

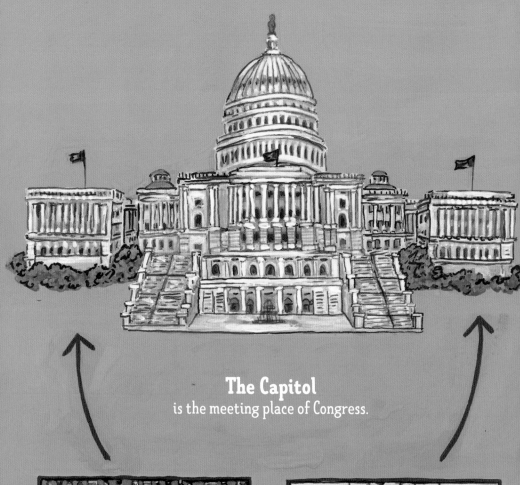

The Capitol
is the meeting place of Congress.

435 U.S. Representatives   100 U.S. Senators

— 8 —

AT THE CAPITOL

You may have seen pictures of the U.S. Capitol, the building that has two long wings with a great white dome in the center. This is the meeting place of Congress, the men and women who make national laws. This is where our leaders give speeches, hold fiery debates, and make history with their votes. At one end of the Capitol is the Senate chamber, where there are desks for one hundred senators—two from each state in the union. At the other end is the chamber of the House of Representatives, with long benches that seat 435 members. As you can tell from the name, the House of Representatives represents the people of the country more directly than the Senate does. Each state has a different number of members in the House, according to the number of people in it. California, which has more people than any other state, sends fifty-

A senator giving a speech

three representatives to Washington, while Alaska, Delaware, Montana, North Dakota, South Dakota, Vermont, and Wyoming send only one each.

Federal laws are made in the same way as in the state legislature. Before people urge their members of Congress to pass a bill, they should remember that the law will apply not only to their own state and district but also to the entire country. What seems good to you might not be good for the rest of the nation.

The White House
is where the president lives and works.

Oval Office

Franklin D. Roosevelt was president from 1933 to 1945.

—9—

THE WHITE HOUSE

Now that we have watched the mayor at City Hall and visited the governor in the Statehouse, we're ready to meet the most powerful leader of them all—the president. From the Oval Office in the White House, the president looks out for the welfare of the United States. He or she makes sure our nation's laws are obeyed, commands our army and navy, chooses judges and other officials, and sends ambassadors to live in the capitals of other countries.

In all this, the president works with Congress. When the president selects officials, he or she needs the approval of Congress, and when the members of Congress make laws, they need the president's approval. If the president disapproves of a bill, he or she can veto it, like a governor does.

The president rarely visits Congress. But every January, he or she goes to the Capitol to give the State of the Union address. Speaking not just to the House and Senate but also to all of us watching on our screens, the president reports on how the country is doing and suggests ways to make it better.

Although our presidents are more powerful than kings are these days, they serve a term of just four years and may be reelected only once. This wasn't always the rule. My husband, Franklin Roosevelt, was elected four times, during the years when America faced many challenges, including a world war. But Congress decided it wasn't a good idea to have the same person in charge of the country for so long.

Besides being one of the most important people in the world, the president is also one of the busiest. About 150 years ago, there was so little going on at the White House that the president's assistants used to play croquet on the lawn while they waited for the next mail delivery. That couldn't happen now. One president had thirty thousand people

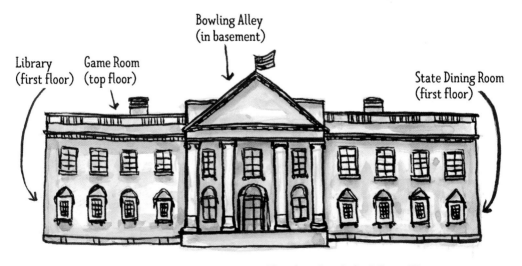

Bowling Alley
(in basement)

Library
(first floor)

Game Room
(top floor)

State Dining Room
(first floor)

North side of the White House

call on him in his first month. And he probably had to shake hands with them all!

Every day the president gets tens of thousands of letters and emails from all over the country, and answers as many as possible. Like the governor, he or she may be asked to pardon people who have broken the laws. The president makes a great many speeches, too, and hosts ceremonies at the White House and only now and then has time to see friends and have a little time off. He or she has to decide not only what's right for the United States, but also how we should deal with people in other parts of the world. This last duty is a very important one, because if we are not wise, just, and kind in our dealings with other governments, we may find ourselves making enemies instead of friends.

As you can see, the leader of our nation has to work hard, like most other Americans. But he or she gets satisfaction from doing a great deal for the country.

Now, about the vice president. He or she is chosen by the candidate for president, and they are elected as a team. The vice president advises and assists the president with certain duties, and sometimes presides over the Senate, casting a vote in the case of a tie.

If you're ten years old, you can run for president in twenty-five years. You must be a natural-born citizen of the United States, and you must have lived here for fourteen years.

secretary of state,

secretary of the treasury,

attorney general,

and secretary of defense
(*originally called secretary of war*).

But as the country has grown, so has the cabinet.

When Franklin Roosevelt was president, there were ten cabinet members.

—10—

THE PRESIDENT HAS FIFTEEN SECRETARIES

How can the president find out about the important things that are happening all over the country and around the world? He or she does it with the help of a cabinet. No, not the kind you're thinking of. This cabinet is made up of experts chosen by the president and approved by the Senate.

The cabinet members are some of the highest-ranking people in government. They're in the line of succession to lead the nation, if something were to happen to the president, vice president, and heads of Congress. Each of them leads a huge executive department. But powerful as they are, neither the president nor his secretaries can make a single law for the nation.

The secretary of state is the head cabinet member and sits at the president's right hand at meetings. An expert in foreign affairs, this secretary has the power to make treaties or agreements with about 180 other countries. He or she oversees the Department of State (DOS), including a staff of undersecretaries for political affairs, human rights, arms control, and other issues. Our ambassadors and consuls in U.S. embassies all over the world are part of the DOS, too. The ambassadors represent our nation to foreign governments, and the consuls look out for our citizens who live abroad. If you leave the United States, you'll need to get a little book called a passport from our Department of State.

The secretary of the treasury heads the department that takes care of our money. It's a tremendous job to manage the government's bank accounts and to make the coins and bills we use! At the U.S. Treasury's mints in Denver and Philadelphia, tens of millions of metal slugs are pressed into coins each day. Paper money, made of linen and cotton, is printed at the Bureau of Engraving in Washington, D.C., and in Fort Worth, Texas. Most of the crisp new bank notes take the place of worn-out bills for one, five, ten, and twenty dollars, which get mangled or torn after about six years.

The Treasury no longer issues bills for five hundred, one thousand, ten thousand, or one hundred thousand dollars—but you can still see them in museums.

The secretary of defense makes sure our armed services are ready to defend the country on land, in the air, and in the water. He or she runs the Department of Defense (DOD), headquartered in the Pentagon at Arlington, Virginia. The DOD is the largest federal organization, and the largest employer in the world. Most defense workers are active-duty servicemen and servicewomen, but some are spies who gather information to keep us alert to threats from other countries.

The attorney general and the Department of Justice (DOJ) prevent crime and enforce federal laws. The eyes of the DOJ are the men and women who work for the Federal Bureau of Investigation (FBI). This department also brings accused criminals to trial and runs the federal prison system, in which the guilty ones may serve their time.

That makes four cabinet positions, and they are the original ones established by George Washington. As the country has grown, so has the cabinet. Today it includes secretaries of the Agriculture, Commerce, Health and Human Services, Homeland Security, Labor, Transportation, Education, Energy, Housing and Urban Development, Interior, and Veterans Affairs departments. The vice president is part of the cabinet, too, so that makes sixteen members in all. You can read more about them on the following chart.

THE OTHER CABINET POSITIONS (added after 1797)

Secretary of Agriculture
Helps the farmers and farming companies grow and sell their crops, does food safety inspection, looks after about 190 million acres of national forests.

Secretary of Commerce
Promotes business and job opportunities. Oversees patents and trademarks, our coastal waters (including national fisheries), weather reporting, and technology. Counts the number of people in the United States (the Census).

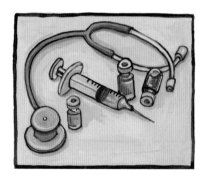

Secretary of Health and Human Services
Conducts medical research, prevents outbreaks of disease, regulates foods and drugs. Provides financial aid to low-income families and protects against child, domestic, and drug abuse.

Secretary of Homeland Security
Works to prevent terrorist attacks and runs the Secret Service. Manages citizen and immigration services. Investigates counterfeit money. Plans and prepares for natural disasters.

Secretary of Labor
Responsible for the welfare of working people, including their salaries, the health and safety of their workplaces, equal opportunity for jobs, and all their other rights.

Secretary of Transportation
Responsible for a fast, safe, efficient transportation system for people and for goods. Maintains federal highways and investigates plane crashes and other transportation accidents.

Secretary of Education

Sets up guidelines for education. Helps local communities meet the needs of their students. Helps pay for college and prepare graduates for jobs.

Secretary of Energy

Develops energy systems that are not too expensive or harmful to the environment. Also responsible for nuclear energy and nuclear weapons technology.

Secretary of Housing and Urban Development

Oversees programs to help Americans with affordable housing, home-ownership programs, housing assistance for low-income families, and help for the homeless.

Secretary of the Interior
Manages and protects most of our public lands and natural resources, including minerals, wildlife refuges, and national parks. Handles our affairs with tribal nations, and America's island territories.

Secretary of Veterans Affairs
Responsible for medical care, benefits, and support for veterans.

Vice President
Warren G. Harding was the first president to include his vice president in cabinet meetings on a regular basis. Franklin D. Roosevelt did the same, as has every president since then.

The U.S. Treasury
collects taxes on things like

income,

tobacco,

airplane travel,

and gasoline.

—11—

WHO PAYS THE BILLS?

Who pays the garbage collectors? Who pays for the new fire truck? Who pays your teacher, the governor, the senators and representatives, and all the people working for us in Washington?

Everyone in the country pays in one way or another. In cities and counties, people who own land or buildings pay a local property tax once a year. In most states, customers are

S	M	T	W	Th	F	S
APRIL					1	2
3	4	5	6	7	8	9
10	11	12	13	14	15 $	16
17	18	19	20	21	22	23
24	25	26	27	28	29	30

charged a sales tax on the things they buy from stores. Some states charge a tax on the land that people inherit or on the amount of money that they earn, called income.

On April 15,* a day most grown-ups don't look forward to, the federal government collects its own income tax. By now, you can guess where this money goes—into the U.S. Treasury. The Treasury also collects taxes on certain items bought in other countries and

* If the 15th falls on a weekend or holiday, then the taxes are due on the next day that is not a weekend or holiday.

things like tobacco, gasoline, and airline travel. Most federal taxes keep the government running, but one of them—the payroll tax—is used to pay people when they retire or when they're too sick to work.

Rich or poor, we should all benefit by what the government does. This means we should all pay our reasonable share of taxes.

—12—

WE, THE PEOPLE

Who has given these powers to the president, to the cabinet members, and to Congress? We, the people of the United States. Long ago, just after the Revolutionary War, a number of our leaders decided that the thirteen states should be joined into one country with the same laws for all. George Washington was among them; so were Benjamin Franklin, James Madison, and Alexander Hamilton.

They and many others were sent to Philadelphia and spent months working on a plan. They created a federal government with three branches: legislative (the Congress), judicial (the judges and courts), and executive (the president and his or her officials). The founders put this plan on a piece of paper, which is still kept in Washington at the Library of Congress, where you may see it. The document is called the Constitution. It begins:

WE, THE PEOPLE OF THE UNITED STATES.

We owe a great deal to the writers of our Constitution. You can tell they did their work well by how long this plan has lasted. Made more than 230 years ago, it still meets our needs, and it does as well for fifty states as it did for thirteen.

But the Constitution is never finished. One very wise thing about it is that a change or

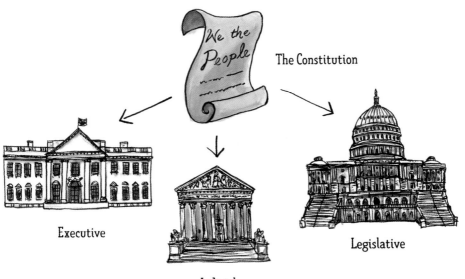

The Constitution

Executive

Judicial

Legislative

addition can be made if there are enough people who wish to have it done. These new parts are called amendments. In the past, several of these changes were made after people sent petitions, gave speeches, wrote articles and pamphlets, and in some cases held parades and protest marches. In large part, this is why we have the Thirteenth Amendment, which abolished slavery, and the Nineteenth Amendment, which granted women the right to vote.

Though you don't often hear about the Constitution, it spells out your basic freedoms and affects you every day.

Judge

Jury

Lawyer

Defendant

Juvenile court

District court

Supreme Court

—13—

WHAT DOES THE JUDGE DO?

We have many judges and many kinds of courts, from the Supreme Court in Washington, down to the local courthouse, where minor lawsuits may be settled.

If children are accused of wrongdoing, they're taken to juvenile courts. The judge explains the criminal charges, decides whether to keep the youths in custody, and determines how to keep them out of trouble. In any court where judges work, their job is to make sure that people are given a fair and proper trial.

The judge doesn't always decide whether a person is to be punished. People who have committed serious crimes have their cases tried in the higher courts before a jury. A jury is a group of twelve persons chosen from the area where the court is located.

U.S. Supreme Court Building

After hearing about the case from lawyers and from witnesses—people who know about it—the jury decides whether the accused is guilty. If the verdict is guilty, then the judge decides what the punishment will be.

Only the most serious cases are brought before the Supreme Court. It has nine judges, called justices, appointed for life by the president and approved by the Senate. Sitting behind a long table in their black robes, they listen to lawyers present their arguments and they ask questions. The Supreme Court justices decide what laws mean, and whether the U.S. Constitution allows them. They have one of the country's most important jobs— they're the guardians of our highest laws.

1. At least 30 days before Election Day, register to vote.

2. On Election Day, arrive at the polling place and receive a blank ballot.

3. Enter a voting booth to mark your ballot in private.

4. Choose your candidates and mark your ballot.

5. Have your marked ballot counted.

6. Congratulations! You voted!

—14—

WHEN YOU GROW UP TO VOTE

Soon, you'll play a part in all of this. When you're eighteen, you'll use your greatest power as an American citizen. You'll help choose the leaders of the government. You'll make decisions that will affect police officers, teachers, doctors, lawyers, judges —and everyone else in your city, state, and country. You'll vote! Marking your ballot is one of the most important—and exciting— things you'll ever do.

You can cast your vote in many ways . . .

Punch card

Electronic voting

Voting lever machine

Paper ballot

As a new voter, you'll be invited to some parties—political parties. You can choose to be an independent voter, or you can join the Democrats, the Republicans, or a smaller party.

The parties have millions of members, but most of their work is done by county, state, and national committees. These groups help members select candidates for president, governor, mayor, and other offices. In some cases, they may recommend how to vote on state laws.

You may be guided by the choices of your party, but you should also learn, on your own, the facts about the issues and the candidates. You need to consider not just your own needs, but also the needs of your neighbors and even people you've never met—all of us in this great nation. When Election Day comes, you should know who and what you're voting for.

To vote, you must register in advance. You must tell your age and where you live. If you were born in the United States or have chosen it for your country, if you have lived long enough in one place, if you can read and write, and if you're at least eighteen, then you'll qualify.

How long will it be until you grow up to vote?

Your Vote

will help choose the leaders of

THE CITY

MAYOR

THE COUNTY

COMMISSION

TOWN   BOROUGH   VILLAGE

THE STATE

SENATE   GOVERNOR   ASSEMBLY

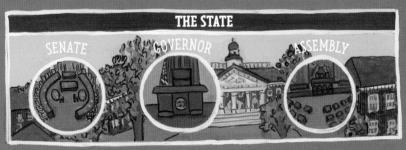

THE NATION

SENATE   PRESIDENT   REPRESENTATIVES

MORE ABOUT OUR GOVERNMENT

Constitutional Amendments and the Years They Were Ratified

The first ten amendments, known as the Bill of Rights, were ratified in 1791.

1. Ensures freedom of religion, of speech, of the press, of peaceful assembly; right to petition government for redress of grievances

2. Grants the right to keep and bear arms (to own guns) in order to maintain a well-regulated militia

3. Prohibits the forced housing of soldiers in citizens' homes

4. Protects people from unreasonable searches and seizures of their property

5. Grants the right against self-incrimination (meaning that you cannot be forced to testify against yourself or be tried twice for the same crime)

6. Grants the right to a fair and speedy trial by jury

7. Grants the right to a trial by jury in a civil or private (not criminal) case

8. Prohibits excessive fines or bail, and cruel or unusual punishment

9. Says that nothing spelled out in the Constitution can be used to prohibit amendments to it

10. Says that powers that have not been granted to the federal government in the Constitution are reserved to the states or to the people

Amendments that were later ratified

11. Prohibits states from being sued by out-of-state citizens or foreigners outside state borders (1795)

12. Revises presidential election procedures (1804)

13. Abolishes slavery and involuntary servitude except as punishment for a crime (1865)

14. Defines what it means to be a U.S. citizen and prohibits states from reducing citizens' privileges (1868)

15. Gives men the right to vote regardless of race, color, or whether they had been slaves (1870)

16. Gives the federal government the right to collect income tax (1913)

17. Establishes direct election of senators by popular vote (1913)

18. Prohibits manufacture or sale of alcohol (1919)

19. Grants women the right to vote, called women's suffrage (1920)

20. Spells out details on the terms of office for Congress and the president (1933)

21. Repeals the Eighteenth Amendment (1933)

22. Limits the president to a maximum of two terms or ten years (1951)

23. Gives Washington, D.C., representatives in the Electoral College (1961)

24. Prohibits the requirement of paying a poll tax in order to vote (1964)

25. Defines presidential succession if something should happen to the president (1967)

26. Sets the national voting age at eighteen (1971)

27. Prohibits laws that change congressional salaries from taking effect until the start of the next session of Congress (1992)

Highlights in the History of Voting Rights

The original Constitution allowed states to be in charge of voting eligibility and elections. At first, only white men who owned property could vote, and in some areas there were religious requirements, too.

Many years passed before the right to vote was guaranteed to all Americans regardless of their race, gender, or religion. To persuade Congress to change the voting laws, people wrote letters, gave speeches, and held rallies and marches. Activists went on hunger strikes, faced jail, or stood up to beatings; some were even killed. Great sacrifices were made for the right to vote, our most cherished power as American citizens.

Voting Rights Timeline

1860   By this year, most states no longer require voters to own property or practice a certain religion. Most white men over twenty-one can vote.

1870   The Fifteenth Amendment declares that "the right of citizens of the United States to vote shall not be denied or abridged by the United States or by any State on account of race, color, or previous condition of servitude."

1890 Native Americans can become citizens by application.

1920 Women are granted the right to vote.

1924 Native Americans born in the United States automatically become citizens, which gives them the right to vote. However, it will be years before every state allows them to do so.

1943 Chinese immigrants are granted the right to citizenship and to vote.

1962 New Mexico becomes the last state to allow Native Americans to vote.

1964 Poll taxes (once required for voting in some states) are repealed.

1965 The Voting Rights Act prohibits election practices that deny the right to vote to citizens because of their race or ethnicity.

1971 The Twenty-Sixth Amendment lowers the voting age to eighteen.

1975 Voting Rights Act provisions are extended. Non-English speakers must be given assistance in voting.

1990 The Americans with Disabilities Act ensures that polling sites have services for persons with disabilities.

Checks and Balances

The founding fathers wanted to make sure that our leaders could not act like kings, imposing rules without consent from the people. So the Constitution has a system of checks and balances. Each branch of government can check (that is, restrain or control) the power and influence of the others.

For example, Congress proposes laws, but the president can veto them. If Congress passes a bill by overriding the veto, the Supreme Court can still decide that the law is unconstitutional. The president appoints judges to the Supreme Court with the approval of Congress—but the Supreme Court has the power to declare acts of Congress and executive orders to be unconstitutional.

One of the legislative branch's greatest checks is the power to impeach. If the president is suspected of treason, bribery, high crimes, or misdemeanors, the House of Representatives can bring forward charges of impeachment. The Senate puts the president on trial, and the Chief Justice of the United States presides.

We, the people, have power over our leaders, too—by choosing whether or not to reelect them.

Gerrymandering

You've seen that political parties select presidential candidates. They also play a large role in our elections—through a process called redistricting. Every ten years, when the nation's population is counted, state legislatures are allowed to create new boundaries for congressional districts. These districts can be any shape or size, as long as they contain around the same number of eligible voters. The majority party in the legislature can draw up districts in a way that will benefit its candidates. This is called gerrymandering.

When gerrymandering districts, state legislatures look at statistics—at party affiliation, income level, race, and ethnicity. If they want to limit the power of a certain race, because this race is likely to vote for the opposite party, they can "pack" minority voters together in fewer districts. In a recent legal case, the Supreme Court found this to be unconstitutional. There are likely to be other lawsuits arguing that gerrymandering is unfair, but its unfairness can be hard to prove.

1. Let's imagine an area with 21 households. You can see that more than half of the voters are blue.

 12 are registered to vote in the Blue party.

9 are registered to vote in the Purple party.

2. Now look at the example below. In each of the three districts more than half the votes are blue, just like #1. During an election, each district would elect a candidate from the Blue party. Result: Blue party wins all three districts.

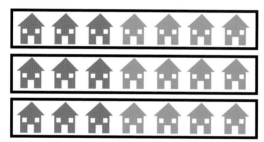 3 Districts:

3 have more Blue voters.

0 have more Purple voters.

Blue wins all districts.

3. Or, the three districts could look like this. At election time, the districts with more Purple voters would elect a Purple candidate, and the district with more Blue voters would elect a Blue one. Can you count the purple and blue voters in each district?

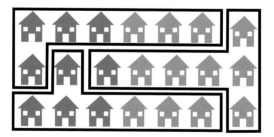 3 Districts:

2 have more Purple voters.

1 has more Blue voters.

Purple wins the majority of districts.

Result: The Purple party wins the majority (2 out of 3) of the districts, even though most of the voters in the whole area are blue.

The Electoral College

It may surprise you to know that while our Congress is elected directly by the people, our president is not.

When voters mark their ballot for president and vice president on Election Day, the vote actually goes to an elector. The electors—who are selected beforehand by the political parties—are known together as the Electoral College.

In the Electoral College system, each state has the same number of electors as they do members of Congress, and the District of Columbia has three. About a month after Election Day, these delegates meet to cast their votes. In Maine and Nebraska, the state's electoral votes can be divided among the candidates. In the other states, the candidate who wins the popular vote receives all that state's electoral votes. To become president, a candidate must receive 270 electoral votes out of 538 possible.

Four of our presidents have won the electoral vote without winning the majority of votes cast nationwide (also known as the "popular vote"). Critics of the Electoral College think our presidents should be elected by the popular vote. Supporters believe that the Electoral College protects the interests of rural states with lower populations.

MORE ABOUT ELEANOR ROOSEVELT

It is not so much the powerful leaders that determine our destiny as the much more powerful influence of the combined voice of the people themselves.

—Eleanor Roosevelt, *Tomorrow Is Now* (1963)

Eleanor Roosevelt loved her country. As an experienced politician—and as a politician's wife—she knew how government worked. She wanted young people to grow up to make smart decisions on Election Day. That's why she wrote this book.

She was born Anna Eleanor Roosevelt on October 11, 1884, in New York, but her family called her by her middle name. Eleanor's father came from a family of prominent public figures: her grandfather was a businessman and philanthropist, and her uncle Theodore was a future U.S. president. As a wellborn girl in a civic-minded family, Eleanor was taken to the poor parts of the city to do small acts of charity. Though she was timid and orphaned by the age of nine, the young Eleanor was not entirely unhappy. She loved reading and spending time in nature, and she attended Marie Souvestre's finishing school in London, where she became a popular adviser to the younger girls.

Eleanor voting in 1936

In 1905, Eleanor married her fifth cousin Franklin Roosevelt. She raised a family (six children in all, five of whom lived to adulthood), ran a large household, and gave Franklin advice and support throughout his political career, starting with his 1910 election to the New York Senate. As Eleanor took on more responsibility, she grew more confident and eager to enter public life. During World War I, she did her part by volunteering for the Red Cross and the Navy League.

In the 1920s, Eleanor became a leader in her own

right. She wrote newsletters for the League of Women Voters, and then, while her husband was recovering from polio, she worked for the Women's Division of the New York State Democratic Committee and the Women's Trade Union League. With other female leaders of the Democratic Party, she helped establish the Todhunter School in New York City, where she taught American history, literature, and current events. When Franklin was elected governor of New York, Eleanor remained active by helping him inspect hospitals, prisons, and other institutions.

It was as First Lady of the United States that Eleanor made her greatest contributions. Despite her natural shyness, she constantly went out in public to support her husband's presidency. She visited cities and farmlands across the country, checking on federal programs and later reporting to Franklin with observations and suggestions. During the Great Depression, she offered the country reassurance in her many speeches, magazine articles, newspaper columns, and radio broadcasts. She lobbied for the rights of poor and marginalized people—in particular, tenant farmers, migrant workers, women, young people, and black people. Though some of Eleanor's views were controversial, she was widely admired for her courage and commitment. She remains the most active First Lady in American history.

After Franklin's death, Eleanor was involved in

many social and humanitarian causes. She was a delegate to the newly created United Nations, where she headed the committee that created the Universal Declaration of Human Rights. During John F. Kennedy's presidency, she served as chair for the Commission on the Status of Women. She died on November 7, 1962.

Eleanor Roosevelt on Citizenship

Eleanor believed that for a democracy to be strong, its citizens must be informed and educated. She thought the best way to learn about government was to attend town halls and meetings:

> *As you progress in interest from local questions to national problems and international situations each step deepens your interest and increases your knowledge. You will discover, to your astonishment, that within a few years time you will have made yourself a discriminating citizen, able to know what you have a right to expect from a candidate, at whatever level.*

—Eleanor Roosevelt, *You Learn by Living* (1960)

During her time as First Lady, when millions of Americans were jobless and World War II broke out in Europe, Eleanor's ideas about citizenship changed. She believed it was the duty of every American to take action to protect democracy. In a radio broadcast on June 20, 1940, she said, "No matter how limited your time or talents, you can give what you have to give to your country by knowing your community and advocating such laws as will help make democracy worthwhile for every individual. The diligent living of your citizenship, from day to day, may mean success for democracy in the world of the future, or absolute failure for our ideals."

Eleanor urged people to get involved in local issues, and to express their opinions to elected officials. Then, she wrote in *The Moral Basis of Democracy* (1940), we'd have a government that "in every way represents the best thought of all the citizens involved. In such a democracy a man will hold office not because it brings certain honors and considerations from his constituents, but because he has an obligation to perform a service to democracy."

Eleanor lived long enough to see the struggles and victories of the modern civil rights movement and other causes. She knew there was much more work to be done, and she encouraged young people to participate. Political action is both necessary and rewarding, she said.

We have to take a new look at ourselves, at what our kind of government requires of us, at what our community needs from us; and then prepare to take a stand. In the long run there is no more liberating, no more exhilarating experience than to determine one's position, state it bravely, and then act boldly. Action brings with it its own courage, its own energy, a growth of self-confidence that can be acquired in no other way.

—Eleanor Roosevelt, *Tomorrow Is Now* (1963)

FURTHER READING ABOUT ELEANOR ROOSEVELT

Books

Cooney, Barbara. *Eleanor*. New York: Puffin Books, 1st Scholastic Edition, 1999.

Fleming, Candace. *Our Eleanor: A Scrapbook Look at Eleanor Roosevelt's Remarkable Life*. New York: Atheneum Books for Young Readers, 2005.

Freedman, Russell. *Eleanor Roosevelt: A Life of Discovery*. New York: Clarion Books, 1993.

Rappaport, Doreen. *Eleanor: Quiet No More*. New York: Disney-Hyperion, 2009.

Websites

The FDR Presidential Library:
https://fdrlibrary.org/eleanor-roosevelt

The Eleanor Roosevelt Papers Project:
https://erpapers.columbian.gwu.edu/about-project